SCIENCE Magic

in the living room

D0550527

SCIENCE Magic
in the living room

Richard Robinson

Illustrated by Alan Rowe

OXFORD

*These books are dedicated to two households: firstly the one
I grew up in, where Dad, Mum, Anne, John and Philip were for ever
dazzling their gullible youngest with tricks like the ones here.*

*Secondly the household I got for myself later, with Morgan
and Georgia providing a new and demanding young audience
for these same tricks.*

OXFORD
UNIVERSITY PRESS

Great Clarendon Street, Oxford OX2 6DP

Oxford University Press is a department of the University of Oxford.
It furthers the University's objective of excellence in research, scholarship,
and education by publishing worldwide in

Oxford New York

Auckland Bangkok Buenos Aires Cape Town Chennai
Dar es Salaam Delhi Hong Kong Istanbul Karachi Kolkata
Kuala Lumpur Madrid Melbourne Mexico City Mumbai Nairobi
São Paulo Shanghai Taipei Tokyo Toronto

Oxford is a registered trade mark of Oxford University Press
in the UK and in certain other countries

Text copyright © Richard Robinson 1999

The moral rights of the author/artist have been asserted

Database right Oxford University Press (maker)

First published in 1999
This edition 2003

British Library Cataloguing in Publication Data available

ISBN 0-19-911156-1

1 3 5 7 9 10 8 6 4 2

Printed in UK

CONTENTS

INTRODUCTION

All the tricks in this book are self-working – that means you don't have to be a great magician to do them. The 'magic' will be done by Nature.

Magic and science have a lot in common.

Both magic and science can produce wonderful effects that leave us gob-smacked. Audiences always want to work out how a magic illusion works. Scientists try equally hard to understand Nature's tricks,

Magicians use a lot of misdirection – getting the audience to look in one direction while the trick is being done in another; Nature often seems to be doing the same. For thousands of years we thought that the Sun travelled across the sky above us; now we know that the Sun stays put and we do the travelling, so the Sun only seems to move. That's Nature misdirecting us.

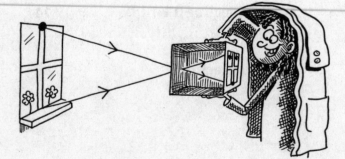

A magician's audiences will often say 'I know how that's done!', when in fact they've got it completely wrong. Scientists often make the same mistake. Two thousand years ago, the Greek philosopher Aristotle had some pretty wrong ideas. For instance, he thought that apples fell from trees because they wanted to. Aristotle's ideas seem crazy nowadays, but for 1500 years everyone thought he was the top banana!

Aristotle's mistakes have been corrected now, but some of the magic in these books still can't be explained even by the best of today's scientists; that makes it doubly magical.

As soon as a scientist finds that an experiment has gone wrong, he starts again, looking and testing and guessing until he gets it right. As you practice these tricks you'll find that they sometimes go wrong, but with a little practice you'll get them right. Soon your tricks will seem as magical to your audience as Nature seems to scientists.

Good luck.

Richard Robinson

CHAPTER ONE
IN THE LIVING ROOM

Your living room is haunted by a ghost – the ghost of Isaac Newton, one of the greatest scientists of all time. Nothing is free from his influence. He helped us to understand: gravity, the force that keeps us stuck to the floor; friction, which stops us from slipping on the carpet; mechanics, which makes all machines run; mathematics, which helped design them; and optics, at the heart of the workings of your TV.

We'll be bumping into him as we make magic with the pocket calculator (Chapter Six) and the pack of cards (page 37). We'll get his help with balancing tricks that defy gravity. We'll take him with us out into space, and we'll settle down to watch TV with him.

Imagine what it was like in Newton's day, 300 years ago. There were no computers, lights, washing machines . . . no electrical appliances – no electricity! No planes, cars, rockets or steam engines. The clock was a new-fangled invention. There was no plastic, nylon, rubber, steel,

 aluminium, fibreglass. There were no scientists to invent them either, although there were some weird folks, alchemists, down in damp and dingy dungeons, mixing together all

sorts of strange things with charms and spells, trying to turn them into gold.

Others – philosophers – spent their lives thinking out how the world worked; why things fell to the ground; why the Moon went round the Earth; what made the seasons, and so on. But because nobody really had the faintest idea, their stories were no better than fairy tales.

Newton was born into this strange world, full of mystical spells and superstitious fairy tales. In his day, the trick that follows would have seemed like truly cosmic magic . . . ah, those were the days!

THRILLING DRILLING

THE EFFECT
The magician makes a glass pass completely through a table.

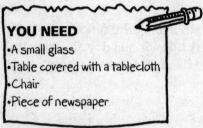

YOU NEED
- A small glass
- Table covered with a tablecloth
- Chair
- Piece of newspaper

TO PERFORM
Perform this trick sitting at the table, preferably over a carpet – just in case the glass drops onto the floor during the performance. Tell the audience that you can turn the glass into a magic thriller-driller, which will drill right through the table. Place the glass on the table, quite close to the edge, and press the newspaper all round it so it hugs the shape of the glass.

Watch the glass expectantly for a few seconds.
No signs of drilling? Pick it up to check the table.
When you've checked, put the glass back. Do this
again twice.

> Important note
> Pick the glass up the same way each time. Don't lift it far
> off the table; just glide it over the edge so it's hovering
> over your lap, then slide it back.

The third time you check for drilling, let your grip on the
newspaper loosen slightly, so the glass drops out on to
your lap. If you are holding it low enough, nobody will
notice. The newspaper will hold the shape of the glass
while you put it back on the table. Now say, *'I think it'd
better give it a hand.'*

Slap your hand down on the newspaper, flattening it.
At the same time, reach under the table as if catching
something, and bring up the glass. The noise of the
slap will give your audience a shock, but not such a
shock as the appearance of the glass from beneath
the table.

WHAT HAPPENED

The mysterious force of **gravity** was your assistant
in this trick, as it will be in many of the tricks that
follow. When you loosened your grip on the glass,
it was gravity that quickly pulled it downwards
into your lap.

Magicians often do tricks that 'defy' gravity, such as
levitation (people floating in the air), the Indian Rope
Trick (climbing up a rope 'hanging' in the air), balls
which float in the air and juggle themselves . . . But
what exactly is gravity? And how does it work?

NEWTON AND THE APPLE

The funny thing is that until Isaac Newton came along, nobody knew that gravity existed. That's not to say that everyone was just hanging around until then, waiting for gravity to be invented. They just had the wrong idea.

O.K. Jump!

When, one day in 1665, the 23 year-old Isaac Newton settled down for a little think under an apple tree, the best story about why things dropped to the ground was the one told by the great Greek philosopher Aristotle, who lived 2,000 years earlier.

Aristotle said that things dropped because they wanted to. Apples fell out of trees because they had a deep desire to return to where they came from – the Earth.

As Newton sat, gazing at the apples up in the tree, he suddenly realised that Aristotle had got it completely the wrong way round. The apples had no desire to do anything; they were perfectly happy to just sit there. But they were being pulled by an invisible force – the force of gravity.

Such a simple thought – but it turned science on its head. Suddenly there was an explanation for everything – why the Moon went round the Earth, why the Earth went round the Sun, why they were all round in the first place.

It even solved the problem of Galileo's balls.

GALILEO'S MAGIC BALLS

Galileo Galilei lived 100 years before Newton. Like Newton, he wanted to work out why things fell to earth. He did a series of experiments and found something rather curious: heavy things fall at the same rate as light things. This didn't seem right. Everyone knew that heavy things dropped faster than light things. It was common sense.

On the other hand, nobody had actually tested it yet. In that kind of world, testing things by experiment was considered unfair. Only spoil-sports would ruin a good scientific truth by actually trying it out.

But they do reach the ground at the same time!

Nobody believed Galileo when he told them they'd got it wrong, so he did a simple demonstration. He climbed to the top of the Leaning Tower of Pisa with two balls: one heavy and one light. He dropped them at the same time.

They hit the ground at the same time.

If Galileo expected everyone to thank him for putting them right, he couldn't have been more mistaken. He was hounded by the old fogies all his life: they believed he was in league with the devil! His demonstration seemed like black magic, because it defied 1,000 years of traditional thinking. A hundred years later, Newton's brand new theory of gravitation finally proved Galileo right.

With any luck you won't be drummed out of town when you do the next trick.

THE GRAVITY OF THE SITUATION

THE EFFECT
Only the magician can drop a piece of paper and a coin so that they both hit the ground at the same time.

YOU NEED
- A large coin
- Two pieces of paper cut slightly smaller than the coin

TO PERFORM
Ask the audience if anyone reckons they can drop a coin and a piece of paper at the same time, from the same height, so that they both hit the ground at the same moment. Show how hard it is by dropping them side by side: the paper flutters down seconds behind the coin. (Have you proved Galileo wrong? Read on . . .)

The answer is to screw the paper up into a tiny ball. Drop the ball of paper with the coin and they both hit the ground at the same time.

Now can anyone do it without screwing up the paper?
Place the paper on the back of the coin, then drop them
both. They hit the ground at the same instant.

WHAT HAPPENED

At first the paper fell slowly because it was buffeted by the
air. When it was screwed up small, it was buffeted less, so
it fell faster.

When the paper was given a ride on the back of the coin,
the coin pushed the air out of the way allowing the paper
to fall at its natural speed.

In the 1970s, during one of the Apollo space rocket
missions to the Moon, the astronauts repeated Galileo's
demonstration by dropping a feather and a ball. In the
airless environment, the feather fell like a stone and
landed at the same time as the ball.

BRAIN BAFFLER

So everything falls at the same rate, huh? What about this teaser. . .

A gun is positioned about three 3 m above the ground, pointing horizontally (flat). At the same time as it's fired, a ball is dropped from the same height as the gun. Which hits the ground first, the ball or the bullet?

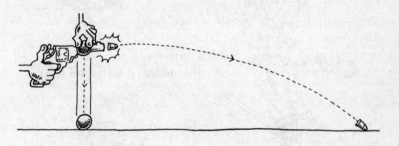

Answer: Incredibly, they both land at the same time, although the bullet is a mile further on. Just as soon as it leaves the gun barrel, gravity starts to pull it down. So regardless of speed, Galileo rules!

CHAPTER TWO

CENTRES OF GRAVITY

Something's **centre of gravity** is the point about which its weight is centred.

If the centre of gravity is over the base on which it stands, the object won't fall.

If it's outside this point, it will keel over.

Most people can tell where an object's 'middle' is. At least, they think they can. Sometimes though, they can be surprised.

For instance, look at a strimmer. Most of the weight is at the back end. When you pick it up, you naturally hold it at the back.

Put it in a box and it begins to look a little strange.

If you balance the box on a wall, it's magic.

BOTTLE BALANCE

This is a trick to do quietly during a meal where there is a tablecloth on the table.

THE EFFECT

The magician makes a bottle stand on one corner, apparently defying gravity.

YOU NEED
- A half-full wine bottle
- A match or cocktail stick

SECRET PREPARATION

When nobody's looking, slip the match under the tablecloth. Do it well before you intend to perform the magic.

TO PERFORM

Tilt the bottle with the corner against the match, as in the picture. You'll find there's a point where it balances. (It will take some time to balance it properly, so do it while everyone's busy.) The match gives just enough support to hold it. You can gently move your hands away and the bottle will stay up, tilted at an impossible angle. (Don't take your hands too far away; it's only the match that's keeping it up. The magic effect will be totally spoiled if the bottle collapses and spills all over the table.) If nobody nudges the table, the bottle will hover there until the others spot it and gawp.

WHAT HAPPENED

This looks like gravity behaving badly. By rights, that bottle should have fallen, but it seemed to hover there.

What it shows is that there are a number of ways to balance an object over its centre of gravity: *we* use only a few of them. Jugglers use a few more . . .

THE COME-BACK TIN

Everyone reckons they know where a tin's centre of gravity is. This trick will really perplex them.

THE EFFECT
The magician makes a tin come when it's called.

YOU NEED
- An empty tin
  (the bigger the better)
- A weight, small but heavy
  (4 big nails would do for a small tin)
- Carpet tape, cool melt glue, or blutac

SECRET PREPARATION
Stick the weight on to the inside wall of the tin using the tape, glue or blutac. Put the tin lid back on (if this has been lost, just make a new one with a piece of card). Work out where the tin's new centre of gravity is (where it balances exactly) and put a tiny mark on the tin so you'll remember.

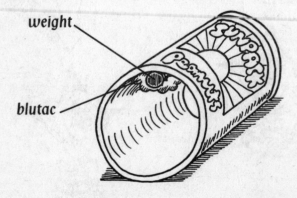

weight

blutac

TO PERFORM

At the start, keep the tin hidden. Say to your audience,
*'I really wanted a dog for Christmas. A dog would have been
nice. Or a cat. Or even a goldfish would have done. Instead of
which, they gave me this.'*

Bring out the tin, and carry on saying, *'I'm not saying that it
isn't a friendly tin. It's not demanding. It needs very little
feeding. Grooming is easy. But somehow it isn't so much fun to
cuddle. It does tricks though. Sit! . . . Good tin! . . . That's about
it, really. Oh yes, and it comes when it's called.'*

Put the tin on its side with the weight at the top, slightly
tipped away from you. Say, *'Here boy!'* and let go of the tin.
It will roll away. Catch it quickly and set it up again the
same way. Much more firmly, say, *'Come here, boy!'* and let
go again. The tin will roll away again. This time replace it
with the weight slightly biased your way, and say, *'Biccies!'*
Now when you release it, the tin will roll towards you.
Pick it up quickly and give it a pat before you put it away.

WHAT HAPPENED

By adding some weight on to one side, the tin's centre of
gravity changed position. With the centre of gravity at the
top, the tin is unstable. It will roll away from or towards
you, depending on which side of the base the weight sits.

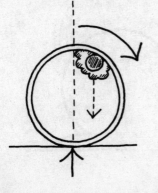 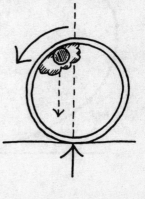

FLUTTER BY, BUTTERFLY

*O*nce again, the centre of gravity is not where people expect.

THE EFFECT
The magician makes a butterfly hover in mid-air.

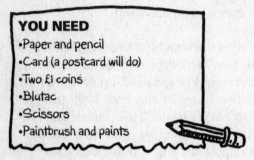

YOU NEED
- Paper and pencil
- Card (a postcard will do)
- Two £1 coins
- Blutac
- Scissors
- Paintbrush and paints

TO MAKE
Fold the paper in half. Draw a half-butterfly shape down the crease, similar to the one here, then cut it out.

fold

When you open the paper up, you will have a symmetrical butterfly stencil. Place it on the card and draw round it, then cut the shape out again. Paint your butterfly, then use the blutac to stick a pound coin under each wing, as far forward as you can.

TO PERFORM
If you balance the tip of the butterfly's nose on the edge of a bookshelf or chair-back, it will hover in the air.

WHAT HAPPENED
With the heavy coins positioned at the front of the butterfly, the centre of gravity has moved right forwards, under its nose.

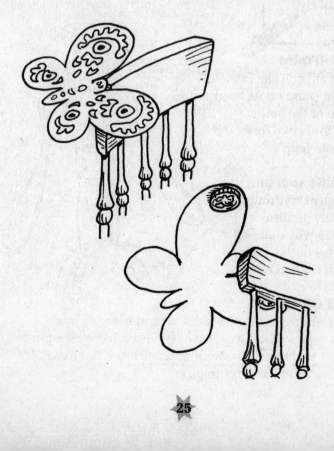

PIN HEADSTAND

In this trick, the centre of gravity moves *outside* the object!

THE EFFECT

The magician makes a pin do a headstand.

YOU NEED
- A bottle
- A pin
- A cork
- Two forks

TO PERFORM

Ask if anyone can make the pin stand on its head, on top of the bottle. Offer them two forks and a cork to help.

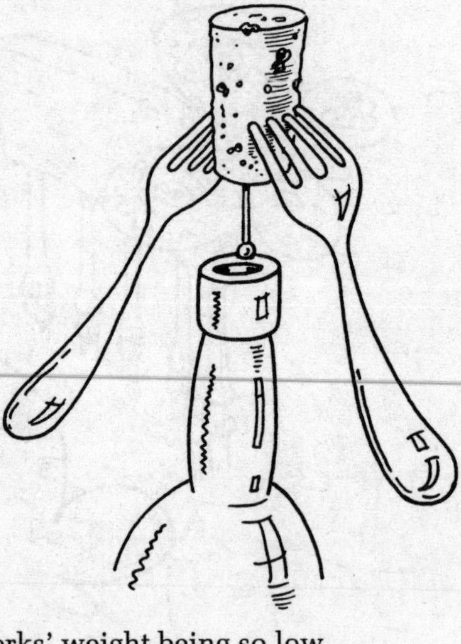

When it's your turn, arrange everything as in the picture. The pin will stand on the edge of the bottle – even if it's rocked.

WHAT HAPPENED

In this arrangement, the forks' weight being so low down means that the centre of gravity is below the pin. It looks as though it's standing on its head, but in fact it's hanging there like a coathanger.

CENTRAL ISSUES

In 1860, the famous tight-rope walker, Charles Blondin, crossed the Niagara Falls in America on a 335 m long tight-rope, 50 m above the rocks. To help stabilise himself, he carried a long pole which bent downwards at the ends. This moved his centre of gravity very close to the wire.

Cargo ships are built to sit low in the water, loaded with goods. When they have unloaded, they bob very high out of the water, running the risk of keeling over. They therefore often have to take on ballast – heavy weights in the bottom of the boat – to move the centre of gravity down below the waterline.

Oil rigs are often not rooted to the seabed, but they're always very stable and solid – even when they're being pounded by the highest seas. This is because the part of the rig that shows above the water is the tiniest tip of a huge structure that has its centre of gravity way down below the surface where the ocean moves a lot slower.

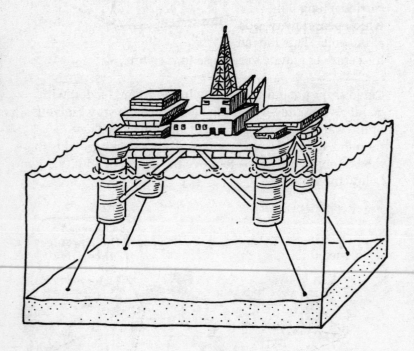

HUP DOG

This is a cracker of a trick. The centre of gravity moves backwards just a little, but this has a big effect.

THE EFFECT
A paper dog lies on the ground, but the magician makes him suddenly sit up and beg.

SECRET PREPARATION
To make the dog, fold a square of paper like this.

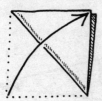 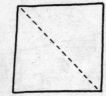 

1 You need a diagonal centre line, so fold the whole sheet over, corner to corner, then unfold it.

2 Fold opposing corners to the centre line, to give a kite shape.

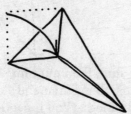 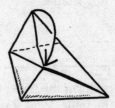

3 Fold the top corner down, to give a triangle.

4 Fold the two top corners in, to give a kite shape.

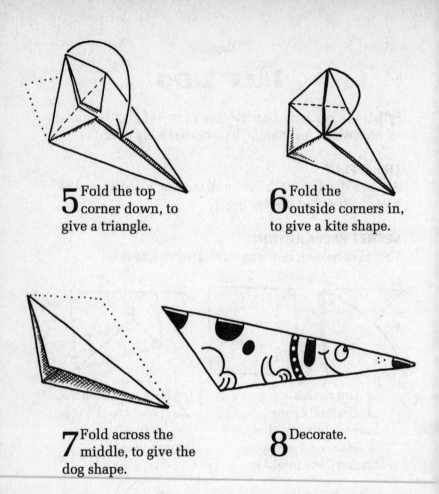

5 Fold the top corner down, to give a triangle.

6 Fold the outside corners in, to give a kite shape.

7 Fold across the middle, to give the dog shape.

8 Decorate.

TO PERFORM

To perform the trick, fold the dog shut, then put him on the table. Wait for a few seconds, then command, *'Hup!'* and he'll jump up on his hind legs. (You'll need to practise a bit beforehand to get your timing just right. If your dog jumps up too quickly, fold him again more firmly. If he's too slow, fold the inner flaps tighter together.)

WHAT HAPPENED

1) After all that folding, most of the paper ended up squashed up in the middle, in front of the pivot – but only just.

centre of gravity

2) As the dog opened out, the centre of gravity moved down towards the table, not in a straight line, but in an arc, which took it slightly further backwards.

3) At the same time, the pivot point moved outwards, not in a straight line, but a curve, which brought it further forwards.

4) These two little changes meant that the centre of gravity was now behind the pivot, so the dog stood up.

CHAPTER THREE
INERTIA

Thanks to Newton, we know how gravity works. We still don't know what gravity really *is* – as soon as we do, there'll be tins of gravity on sale at the local supermarket – but we certainly know that things don't drop because of any inner urge.

In fact, objects don't have any desire to do anything in particular. Transport Newton, apple tree and apple into outer space where there is no gravity, and the apple will stay put forever, hovering by its twig. (You'd better take Isaac a cup of tea and a jammy dodger every now and then, or he won't stay put for long!)

As Newton put it, an object will stay where it is unless an outside force acts on it. This tendency for objects to stay put is called **inertia.**

A magician's tendency to exploit it is called **cunning.**

BOOK HYPNOTISM

This trick relies on inertia for its crafty cunning.

THE EFFECT
The magician hypnotises a pile of books. They stay fast asleep while a sheet of paper is removed from beneath them.

YOU NEED
- Some books
  (not valuable ones)
- A sheet of paper

TO PERFORM
Ask the audience to try to remove a sheet of paper from beneath a book without it moving. They will find it pretty well impossible. Even those who know the right technique will find that the book moves a little.

Tell them that you can hypnotise the book, and not just one, but two . . . three . . . four . . . ten books at once, so they will not notice the paper being taken.

Pile the ten (or however many you're comfortable with) books neatly on top of the paper.
Hypnotise them by

waving your arms over them and saying, *'You are feeling sleepy . . . very sleepy . . . '*. Now yank the paper outwards horizontally, as fast as you can. The books will stay where they are.

WHAT HAPPENED

You'll find that the paper comes quite easily if it's yanked quickly. The faster you pull, the less time the books have to move in response, so the more inertia keeps them still. More books mean more weight and more inertia, so it's actually easier to do the snatch on ten books than one!

Practise the snatch before you perform the trick and it won't take long for you to get quite skilful. There are stories of magicians pulling the tablecloths off tables loaded with entire dinner sets – but don't try that yet!

THE ELBOW SNATCH

Put a coin on your elbow, as in the drawing.

Now try to catch it in one sweep of the hand.

If you're quick enough, you'll be able to grab it before gravity can pull it down too far.

When you have mastered one coin, try with more. How many can you manage?

DRAUGHT SORTING

THE EFFECT
A stack of draughts has to be sorted into white and black.
The magician can do it in ten seconds.

YOU NEED
•Draughts
•A ruler

TO PERFORM
Stack the draughts into a pile, alternating black and
white. Keep the ruler hidden for the moment.

Ask the audience how long they think it should take
to sort them out into white and
black. Then say, confidently,
*'Now, let's see how long it
takes me.'*

Now produce the
ruler, place
it flat on the
table, and slide it
from side to side
like a demented
windscreen wiper.
The white draughts will fly off one
way and the blacks the other.

WHAT HAPPENED
If you're fast enough, the inertia of the draught stack will
keep it in place until all the draughts are sorted.

ARREST THAT CARD!

Inertia is not just for static objects. Newton said that moving things will carry on at the same speed in a straight line unless acted on by an outside force. We'll use that in this next trick.

THE EFFECT
A card is chosen and returned to the pack. The pack is thrown away, but the magician makes the chosen card fly back.

YOU NEED
- Ten playing cards
- 1 m of dark thread
- Dark clothes to perform in, so the thread doesn't show
- Blob of blutac
- Sellotape

SECRET PREPARATION
Sellotape one end of the thread underneath the table just in front of you. Attach a small blob of blutac to the other end.

When it is time to do the magic, you must hold this blob between your fingers, as in the drawing. Keep your hand low, to keep the thread hidden.

TO PERFORM

Say, *'Now I am <u>not</u> going to do a card trick, and this is the card trick I'm not going to do. Would one of you care to step up and take a card.'*

Spread the cards, but keep them close to the edge of the table, to hide the thread.

'Thank you. Now memorise the card and give it back to me.'

Take the card and place it in the middle of the pack, secretly pressing the blutac to the bottom edge. Keep the cards low and keep them spread.

'Now I know where your card is. You know where your card is. But do the cards know where your card is? Let's find out if they can do the card trick for us.' Then say to the cards, *'All right, you may go, all of you but the chosen card!'*

Fling them away upwards to your left. They will all fly off except the tethered one, which falls into your hand.

WHAT HAPPENED

What stopped the tethered card from flying off was the piece of thread. What stopped the other cards, a second or so later, was a little air resistance and a lot of gravity. Without those two, they would have continued flying off forever, straight out towards the stars. So the thread had an effect similar to gravity; it pulled the card back from its natural path.

FIRST CUP IN ORBIT

This is another stunner that defies gravity.

THE EFFECT
The magician takes a drink for a spin on a string and spills nothing.

YOU NEED
- Plastic cup
- An old plastic or tin plate
  (not breakable and as small as you like)
- Water
- 3 pieces of string, each
  about 40 cm long
- Sellotape

SECRET PREPARATION
Arrange the strings around the plate as shown, tied together at the bottom. Then adjust the lengths so they're all the same, and tie them at the top.

TO PERFORM
Fill the cup with water and place the cup on the plate. Hold everything as shown.

Now swing the spinner – slowly at first, then faster and faster, until finally you are spinning it in a circle around your head.

The audience will be
amazed, but not
sprayed (no water will
leave the cup).

Now the task is to stop it. This can be
more tricky, but by slowing down
gradually you can bring the plate
to rest, then take a drink from the
cup to prove it wasn't
stuck down.

WHAT HAPPENED

If you had let go of the string, the plate would have carried
on in a straight line. Instead, the plate was pulled back
continuously by the string. The cup, also wanting to travel
straight, was constantly pulled back by the plate.
Similarly, the water was pulled back by the cup.
Everything was straining outwards but constantly
hauled inwards. The artificial sideways force is
called **centrifugal force.**

Think about when a car turns a tight corner. The inertia of
the passengers carries them straight, but the
sides of the car force them round
the corner. The passengers feel
that they are being pressed
against the side of the car.
That's centrifugal force.

WHY THE TOAST ALWAYS LANDS BUTTER-SIDE DOWN

One of the most important sets of laws in science is Murphy's Laws. Murphy's first law is, 'Anything that can go wrong, will go wrong'. A whole range of other laws follows from this, such as, 'The other queues always move faster than yours'; and 'Things are always found in the last place you look'. Perhaps the most famous of all is 'The toast always lands butter-side down.' Inertia provides the proof of this law.

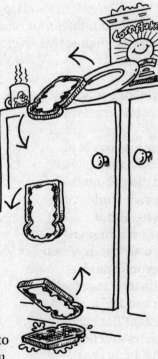

At the point where the toast tips over the edge of the plate, it starts to turn. As it falls, the spin continues by its own inertia, so that by the time it meets the freshly cleaned floor, it has made one half turn – it's upside down. If the floor were further away, the spin would continue and the toast would land butter-side up. The scientific lesson to be learned from this is that you should always wear stilts when making toast.

CHAPTER FOUR
MAGIC IN YOUR BONES

Ever thought how daft it is to have only two legs?
Nobody makes tables or chairs with two legs. How do
they expect us to keep standing without at least three?
Look at babies trying to stand up: wobble, wobble. Give
them an extra leg, and they'd be standing before
you can say, ''Ere, where did you get that extra leg from?'
But when baby starts walking, watch them . . . they tilt
forwards a bit, then a bit more, then they put their foot
out to stop themselves keeling over – and that's baby's
first step!

So walking is actually a process of continuously
almost falling over.

Within a couple of
months, they have
forgotten about this
constant battle with
gravity. But it
continues in secret.
Put your hands round
someone's ankles
while they stand still.
You can feel a
constant flexing of
muscles and tendons
as the body goes
through its continu-
ous routine of
keeping you up.

FOUR WAYS YOU CAN'T KEEP UP

These little tricks reveal the secret ways you keep your balance. They will also fox anyone you challenge to try them.

FORWARDS – BACKWARDS

Stand with your back and heels against the living room wall. Drop a coin on the floor just in front of you. Can you pick it up without falling over? When you bend forwards, your centre of gravity starts to move forwards too. Normally, you'd compensate by sticking your bum further out behind you. But with the wall there, this is impossible, so you tip over.

SIT DOWN – STAND UP

Sit straight up on a chair, with your arms down beside you. Can you get up without using your arms or leaning forwards? Your centre of gravity is over the chair. To stand up, you must move it over your feet. It's impossible to stand up if you don't lean forwards.

LIFT AND TIP

Stand sideways with your shoulder, hips, and foot against the wall. Can you lift your outside foot? To take away one of your two supports, your centre of gravity must be shifted over the other foot. You must either stick part of you through the wall, or collapse.

LOOK BEFORE YOU LEAP

Put your feet together, bend over, and grab hold of your toes with both hands. Can you hop? In order to hop, you have to move your centre of gravity forward ahead of your feet, but you can't do that because you're hanging on to them.

EARS WHERE YOU ARE

The place which tells you
where you are, which way
up you are, what angle
you're at, which way you're
going, and at what speed, is
a tiny organ in the bone just
behind each ear, called the
semi-circular canals. These
are minute tubes full of
liquid, and they rely on the
inertia of the liquid to
register what's happening.

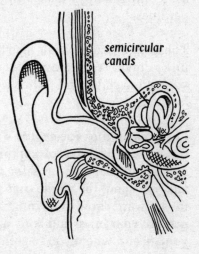

semicircular
canals

You can see how this works
by floating a small piece of paper on top of a cup of water.
Can you move the paper around by rotating the cup? It's
not easy. The water and paper tend to stay where they are,
however much you swizzle the cup.

That's what happens in the semi-
circular canals. Hairs in the canal
wall stick out into the liquid. When
your head moves, the liquid stays
put, so the hairs are bent and the
brain recognises this as rotation.

Nothing's perfect, of course. Spin
the cup around a few times. When
you stop the cup, the water keeps
spinning. This is exactly what
happens when you spin round
a few times.

The fluid in your semi-circular canals keeps on swirling after you've stopped, so while most of you thinks you're static, the inner ear insists you're still spinning – giddiness!

The semi-circular canals also tell you whether you're going up or down. When a car races over a sharp hill, you leave your stomach behind. When a lift sets off, the same happens.

Combine all the movements – up and down, left and right, forwards and backwards, spinning round – and what do you have? That ferry crossing when the sea was so rough and you spent the whole time in the loo! Sea sickness is the outward show of an inner argument, with different parts of your brain and body arguing violently about where you are and where you're going.

Astronauts have to cope with another kind of nausea, because semi-circular canals are used to working with gravity. The brain goes into total dismay mode when

gravity disappears – sickness on the rolling ocean is nothing compared with floating calmly in space.

Your brilliant brain is continuously trying to map the world around you. Stand at one end of the room, take a good look around, then shut your eyes and try to get to the opposite corner. At each step you take, your brain recalculates the position of everything around you, so you can negotiate pretty well right across the room just from memory. It's a truly phenomenal mental feat.

Watch someone drive a car. Motorists extend their senses to fill their new 'virtual' body. They seem instinctively aware of where the back bumper is, how far they are from the car behind, how fast they're . . . Ooops! Well, sometimes we can misjudge things.

Occasionally the body does something that even your brain isn't expecting and can't explain. Scientists use these times to investigate the way the body works. They can also be used by crafty magicians . . .

ARM LEVITATION

THE EFFECT
The magician casts a spell over somebody. Their arm obeys orders and levitates into the air quite of its own accord.

TO PERFORM
Announce that you are going to give the ultimate demonstration of the magic craft of levitation. Choose your subject carefully. They must be prepared to let you have control of their whole body for a short while.

Ask your volunteer to stand right-side on to the wall, nicely relaxed, with their arms down by their side. Keeping their right arm straight, they must try to raise it sideways *through* the wall. While they do this, for about 30 seconds, encourage them to push as hard as possible. You can only be sure of whole-body levitation if they push so hard that the wall moves an inch or so.

After 30 seconds of straining, tell them to stop pushing, turn to the front, shut their eyes, relax completely, and wait. Their arm will float up in the air!

WHAT HAPPENED
The subject's shoulder muscle was straining at the task of pushing the wall down – so hard that it forgot how to stop. Even though the brain stopped sending messages to keep pushing, the muscle remained 'in spasm' for a short while, and the arm rose 'magically.'

CHAPTER FIVE

Friction, Non-Friction

Friction is the resistance that happens when two things move against each other. When you push a table or chair, they put up a bit of a struggle, scraping across the floor. That scraping is caused by friction. (If they put up a lot of a struggle, there's another kind of friction, between you and Mum!)

Friction is as basic to life on Earth as gravity is. For example, holding a frictionless coin would be impossible. It would be so smooth that it would slip through your fingers like a bar of wet soap.

Friction happens because everything has a rough surface.
Yes, everything! Even things that look completely smooth!

This is what soap
looks like close-up . . .

And this is what glass
looks like
close-up . . .

Not as smooth as
you think. At the
microscopic level,
it's like a mountain
range.

A GRIPPING STORY

What would happen if friction disappeared suddenly?

The floor becomes as slippery as an ice rink. You fall to the ground just as your clothes fall off your body, unable to keep a grip on you any longer. All their threads unravel.

The books slither off the shelves onto your head. All the screws and nails in the room slip out of their housings, and the furniture collapses. Everything slides to the lower corner of the room, pulled by gravity.

The bricks in the house can't hold together; the whole lot crashes down and begins to flow down the friction-free road, joining all the other houses in the street as they stream towards the nearest river. Soon the whole town is oozing down the valley, heading for the sea.

The mountains can't stay up without friction between the rocks. Everything collapses. Pretty soon the surface of the whole planet is little more than a slimy gruel of featureless gunge, not unlike that pudding they serve up every now and then at school.

But it tastes better

So next time you're fishing down the back of the sofa, trying to see if the TV control has dropped behind it again, spare a moment to thank your lucky stars for friction.

DROP-STOPPER

The next few tricks depend on friction for their success.

THE EFFECT

A silver ball hangs in the middle of a piece of string. No one touches it, but it drops at the magician's command and it stops when told to.

YOU NEED
• Baking foil
• Thread
• Pencil

SECRET PREPARATION

Screw up the foil into a ball. It should be about 8 cm across. Then use a pencil to poke a V-shaped hole through the ball, first poking in one side, then the other. Next push the thread through. Now, when you hold the thread up vertically, as in the drawing, the ball should slip freely up and down. When you pull gently on the thread, it stops.

TO PERFORM

Say, '*This is one of the mysterious silver apples of Isaac Newton. The apple was never happy with Newton's notions on gravity. It believes that it shouldn't fall because gravity pulls it, but because it wants to.'* Pause for a second, then say, *'OK apple, you can fall now if you want.'* Release your pull a little and the apple will drop. Then say, *'OK apple, stop!'* Tighten the thread, so the apple stops. Do this for as long as you like.

WHAT HAPPENED

Pulling the thread straight rubs it against the tin foil, increasing the friction and preventing gravity from having its way.

Or not. You may have difficulty getting it to work if:

1 The ball is too light. If there isn't enough weight and not enough pull from gravity, the ball will just sit there.

2 The thread is too thin. If it can't provide enough friction, the ball will plummet.

3 The thread is too smooth. Again, there won't be enough friction and the ball will drop.

4 The thread is too thick. There will be too much friction and the ball will stay put.

Engineers have to balance the various forces of weight and friction precisely when designing machinery. So do magicians!

GOB-SMACKING BOTTLE STOPPER

This trick uses something with a great deal of friction to make sure the magic works.

THE EFFECT
The magician picks up a bottle using nothing but a pencil.

YOU NEED
• Dark wine bottle
• Pencil
• Rubber eraser

SECRET PREPARATION
Cut a piece off the rubber and make it into a ball a little smaller than the mouth of the bottle. Slip it into the bottle.

TO PERFORM
Tell your audience you will pick up the bottle using just a pencil.

Hold the bottle and put the pencil in, ever so casually turning the whole lot over as you do. The rubber will drop down next to the pencil in the bottle's mouth. Turn the bottle right side up, let go of the bottom, and the bottle will hover!

WHAT HAPPENED
Rubber is very good at increasing friction. That's why it's used for computer mats, ping-pong bats, under nearly all the electrical equipment in the house, and so on, and so on . . .

STICKING TO THE RULER

This trick plays friction forces against gravity forces in a simple and elegant demonstration.

THE EFFECT

A ruler balances on the index fingers of both of the magician's hands. When the fingers move together, they always meet right in the middle.

YOU NEED

- A ruler (the longer the better) or any long straight object (a piece of wood or a broom handle would do)

TO PERFORM

Balance the ruler on your fingers, as in the drawing. When you move your fingers slowly in towards each other, the smart ruler slides over one finger, then stops to let the other catch up, and so on, until both fingers are in the middle. The question is, can we outsmart the ruler?

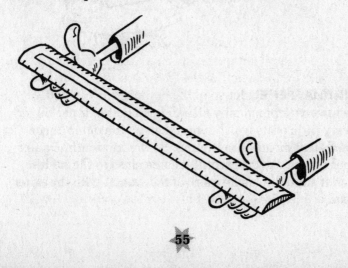

Balance the ruler again, this time with one finger at the edge, as before, but the other very close to the middle. Which finger will get to the middle first? Get everyone to guess before starting off again.

This time the outside finger does nearly all the moving. The two fingers end up in the middle at the same time.

WHAT HAPPENED
The ruler was practically all balanced on the inner finger, so very little of its weight was taken by the outer finger. Less weight means less friction. So the friction-free outer finger had an easy ride until it came close to the middle, when it started to share more of the weight with the other finger.

INVISIBLE CARD TRICK

Use some mucky, yucky stickiness to help your magic.

THE EFFECT

The magician produces an invisible pack of cards. A volunteer takes an invisible card from it, 'memorises' it, turns it upside down and returns it to the pack. The magician produces a real pack and finds the identical card upside down in it.

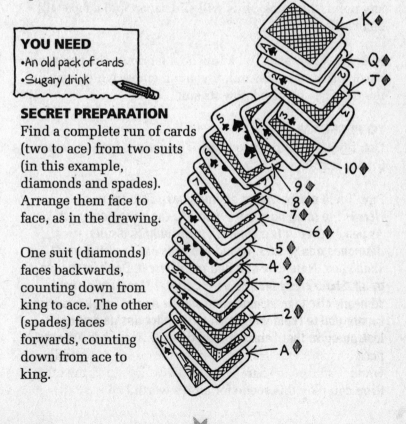

YOU NEED
•An old pack of cards
•Sugary drink

SECRET PREPARATION

Find a complete run of cards (two to ace) from two suits (in this example, diamonds and spades). Arrange them face to face, as in the drawing.

One suit (diamonds) faces backwards, counting down from king to ace. The other (spades) faces forwards, counting down from ace to king.

The pack now has 13 face-to-face pairs. If you spread the cards, you see every second card is face-up, in order (ace to king), and of a single suit. If you turn the pack over, you see the same in the other suit.

Use the sugary drink to stick the face-to-face pairs together. Just wipe a little of it on to each card of the pair and leave out to dry.

Put the pack together and practise fanning the cards. When you spread the pack only the backs should show, because the faces are stuck together. But if you force the cards at any point, the stuck cards will slide apart and a face will be revealed.

Now you are ready. You know how far down the pack any particular number is, and, if you remember which way up the pack is, you also know its suit.

TO PERFORM

Don't bring your cards out yet. The actions here are done totally in mime.

Say, *'I will now perform an imaginary card trick.*
Here is my imaginary pack. I shuffle the imaginary pack.
As you can see, it is a smallish pack: only two suits –
diamonds and spades. Would someone like to pick a card? . . .
Thank you. Now look at it and memorise it. Don't let me see it
at all. Show everyone else your card. . . Meanwhile, would
someone else take the pack and shuffle it? . . . Thank you. Now
I want you to replace the card in the pack upside down. I'll
look away so that I can't see anything . . . Now hand me the
pack.'

(You can play this scene for all it's worth.)

Then say, 'Now, could you please tell me the name of your
card . . .' They say, 'Nine of spades.' Question them, 'Are you
sure that was the name of your card? Do you mind if I check?'
Now produce the pack. Make sure you hold it with spades
face-up.

Don't let them see the bottom of the pack, or the trick is
exposed.

Spread the pack carefully, counting under your breath
until you get to nine, then force that pair apart, revealing
the nine of spades, the only face-up card in the pack.

ACROBATIC ACES

Sometimes you don't want more friction, you want less.
If you want your cards to run smoother, not to stick
together, then dust a little talcum powder between them.
The king of the smooth running machine is oil. Nearly all
of a car engine is covered with oil, which is vital if all the
pistons and wheels are going to move without too much
friction. This trick uses that slippery quality.

THE EFFECT
The magician has a very special pack of cards. Most of
them are lazy, but the aces are frisky.

YOU NEED
- An old pack of cards
- Cooking oil
- Wine glass (the sort with a
  narrow, tapering bowl)

SECRET PREPARATION
The type of glass is important. Test it carefully before
attempting this trick. If a card is bent and pushed into it, it
should stay there, held in by friction against the side. If
you put a line of oil up either side of the glass, then insert
a card so that its edges are against the oily part, it should
pop out, since the friction no longer holds it.

TO PERFORM
Inform the audience that your cards are a bit of a mixed
bunch. Some are quite shy (insert a card into the glass,
where it stays). Some are sleepy (take the first card out and
put in another). Some are plain scared (again replace the

card in the glass with another). And some are pretty wild, such as the aces (insert an ace, this time with its edges against the oily part of the glass.) It'll pop out again, and will keep popping out however much you shove it in.

STICKING POINT - GLUES

The best way to prevent slipping is to use the ultimate friction-maker: glue. But what makes glues glue? What makes sticky things stick?

Glue basically fills holes. As you've seen from looking at soap and glass close-up, even the smoothest things are pretty pitted. Glue pours into the tiny holes and anchors itself there. Scientists are designing a whole range of sophisticated new glues, but some appear quite by accident.

One famous accidental invention was the Post-it. In the laboratories of the giant 3M company, scientists were trying to find a super strong-glue, but things went disastrously wrong and they ended up with a glue so useless it hardly stuck anything to anything. But the laboratory technician didn't want to just throw it away. What about using it to stick temporary labels on things? No one was interested.

Secretly, the technician made up some little packets of these labels and sent them to various departments with a note saying that if they wanted more, they should contact the stores department. Soon the stores department was flooded with requests for more Post-its. 'What are Post-its?' they screamed. 'We've never heard of them!' When the truth came out, the managers realised that their 'useless' glue was actually very useful indeed.

Bigger Than This

THE EFFECT
A volunteer chooses a card, puts it back in the pack, and shuffles the cards thoroughly. The magician puts the cards into an envelope, reaches in, and after a couple of near misses, pulls out the chosen card in a most spectacular way!

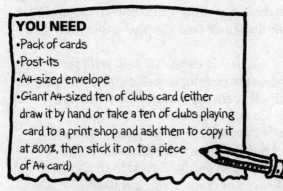

YOU NEED
- Pack of cards
- Post-its
- A4-sized envelope
- Giant A4-sized ten of clubs card (either draw it by hand or take a ten of clubs playing card to a print shop and ask them to copy it at 800%, then stick it on to a piece of A4 card)

SECRET PREPARATION
Use the sticky part of a Post-it to stick a five of clubs and a seven of clubs to the back of the giant card, then put it into the envelope.

To prepare the cards, position the ten of clubs ninth card down in the pack.

TO PERFORM
Ask a volunteer to think of

a number between 10 and 19. Then tell them to add the digits together and subtract the result from their first number. Now they must count that number of cards off the top of the pack. Ask them to show the last card they dealt to everyone in the room except you.

Tell them to replace their card in the pack and shuffle the pack thoroughly. You cannot possibly know what the card is, can you? (Actually, it's the ninth card, the ten of clubs.)

Take the pack off them and drop it into the envelope. Tell them that you can find their card simply by touch.

(A little hint here. Make this seem difficult, with lots of scrabbling around in the envelope, feeling this, dropping that . . . but eventually bringing out the five of clubs.)

Say, 'Is it this one?' (They will say, 'No'.) Say, 'I sense that it's a club . . . am I right?' (They will say, 'Yes'.) Ask, 'Is it bigger than this?' ('Yes,' they reply.) Scrabble some more, then produce the seven of clubs. Ask, 'Is it this?' ('No,' they say.) Ask again, 'Is it bigger than this?' ('Yes,' they reply.) At this point they will begin to think you're floundering. Now is the time to produce the big card and say, 'Well, it can't be bigger than this!'

CHAPTER SIX

CALCULATED CUNNING

At the time when Newton was struggling with the sums needed to calculate how the planets went thundering around the universe, the fastest calculator in the world was the abacus.

Newton had to devise an entirely new kind of maths to help him, called **calculus**. Calculus provided Newton with some useful short-cuts to the answers he needed, and since then it has been a vital tool for mathematicians, scientists and engineers. Without needing to go into calculus, here are some other useful short-cuts you can use.

HANDY CALCULATOR

*T*his will give you an instant nine times table.

Number the fingers of both hands from 1 to 10. Now, say you want to multiply 9 by 7, just bend the 7 finger over. The answer is the number of fingers on the left of the bent-over finger – 6 – followed by the number of fingers on the right – 3 . . . 63!

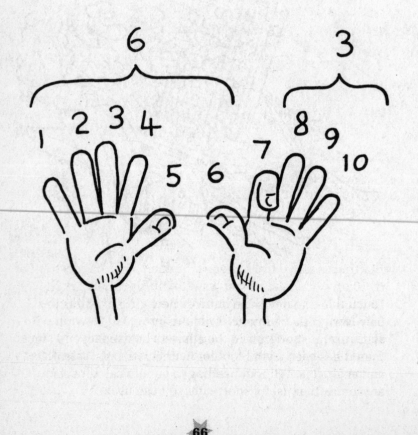

THE FINGER COMPUTER

This one will help with times tables between six and ten.

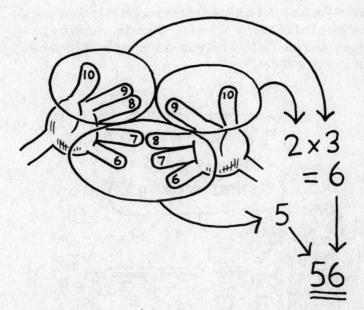

Starting with the little fingers, numbers your fingers from 6 to 10 on each hand. If you want to multiply, say, 7 x 8, touch the 7 finger of one hand to the 8 finger of the other. The lower fingers show how many tens in the answer – 5 in this case – so that's 50. Multiply the top fingers of one hand by the top fingers of the other, 3 x 2 = 6, and add that to the 50, to get 56 – the answer!

The Pocket Calculator

Here are a couple of silly tricks to play on a pocket calculator.

FRACTIONALLY OUT

One of the simplest oddities of the pocket calculator goes like this: divide 100 by 3, then multiply the result by 3. The answer should be what you started with, of course – 100, not 99.999999!

FUELS PARADISE

A friend is thinking of opening a new petrol station in a country where there are no cars. Your calculations tell him whether it's a good idea or not. Punch in these numbers and read the screen upside down after each '='.

$38.07 \times 2 =$

$+ 7657.66 =$

$- 2198 =$

$- 4827 =$

Did you know that over 40 words can be found by looking at calculator screens upside down. Why don't you work out your own magic trick like this one, using these numbers/letters?

1 2 3 4 5 6 7 8 9 0
I   E h S g L B b O

DATE DATA

THE EFFECT

Someone thinks of an important date in the year, then buries it in a mass of sums on the calculator. Yet the magician can find the date in seconds.

TO PERFORM

Ask someone to think of an important date in their life, either a birthday or a public holiday or even a completely invented one. We'll use March 25th as an example.

Without looking, ask them to enter the following on a calculator:

The number of the month (January is 1, through to December, 12)	3
Multiply by 5	15
Add 6	21
Multiply that by 4	84
Add 9	93
Multiply by 5	465
Add the number of the day	490
Add 700	1190

Ask for the calculator back, then quickly enter: − 865 = . The number shown is the date: the last two digits are the day of the month, and the first digit (or digits) is the number of the month. In this case, 1190 − 865 = 325, which is March (the 3rd month), 25th.

MAD MATHS

Whether you are trying to solve a scientific problem or work out a magic trick, you must always expect the unexpected. Here are some silly sums; see if you can solve them. Remember if the answer seems easy, it isn't; if the answer seems hard, it isn't!

1 SHEEPISH QUESTION
Ask someone this sum. You'll be amazed at how wrong they get it.

There are 20 sick sheep in a field. One of them dies. How many are left alive?

2 DAZE IN THE YEAR
Arthur Dubbins had been working for the same company for 30 years. He started there as an apprentice and had never had an increase in pay since. It was time, he thought, to ask for a rise. His manager listened to his plea, then in amazed tones, said, 'Now just a minute, Dubbins. Let's see how much you actually do for me. You work here for 8 hours a day, which is ⅓ of a day. This year is a leap year, so you really only work 122 days out of the 366. You don't work on Saturdays or Sundays, a total of 104 days a year, so that leaves 18 days. You have four bank holidays, leaving 14 days, plus a fortnight's holiday, which leaves . . . gracious, man! You don't work for me at all!'

3 COMPLETELY QUACKERS
Some ducks are walking in a line. There are two ducks in front of a duck, two ducks behind a duck, and a duck in the middle. How many ducks in all?

4 HAVE YOU HERD?

A farmer gave his herd of cows to his three children when he retired. Half was to go to his eldest, ¼ to the middle child, and ⅕ to the youngest. When they checked the herd, they found there were 19 cows. How could they divide them up without slicing them up?

They didn't want to end up with bits of cow each, so they were relieved when their neighbour offered to help. He added his cow to the herd, making 20 in all. Half of that was ten, ¼ was 5, and ⅕ was four – a total of 19. So the neighbour took back his own cow and everyone was happy.

5 EATING DISORDER

A girl had five apples and ate all but three. How many were left?

6 IN THE END IT'S EASY

Can you do this sum in your head?

$$3 \times 4 \times 13 \times 24 \times 67 \times 311 \times 50 \times 2 \times 0 = ?$$

7 THERE MUST BE A CATS

If three cats catch three rats in three minutes, how many cats are needed to catch 99 rats in 99 minutes?

8 PROSE AND CONDIMENTS

A three–volume dictionary sits on a shelf. Each book is an inch thick. A bookworm eats all the way from the first page of volume one to the last page of volume three. How far does it travel? (As you might expect, the answer is not three inches.)

CHAPTER SEVEN

EYE-BOGGLING

Wave a pen in front of the TV screen . . . sorry, wave six pens – where did they come from?

What you see as a continuously moving image on the TV is actually a string of still pictures being flashed on the screen about 30 times a second. With video frame-advance control you can see each individual frame. So your waving pen was caught in a series of flashes, each flash leaving a shadow.

Normally, your brain fills in the gaps between the TV's flashes. This ability of the brain to blend pictures together, called **persistence of vision**, makes it possible for TV to work. Instead of seeing a series of uncomfortable flashes 30 times a second, we see smooth movement. We can do some smooth magic with this . . .

Finding the Right Word

THE EFFECT

Somebody picks a number and performs some simple sums with it on a calculator. The magician hands him a book and says he'll find that number very easily in it. Leafing through the book, he finds a moving dot, which guides him to a particular word. The magician claims that's what he has on the calculator. Indeed, when the calculator is turned upside down, the word appears.

YOU NEED
- An old paperback book (make sure nobody wants it)
- Pocket calculator
- Felt tip pen

SECRET PREPARATION

Look in the book, at around page 20, for the word 'is'. Draw a circle round it. Now turn forward 100 pages and put a big dot just by the right edge of the right page.

If you turn back one page, you should still be able to see that dot faintly through the paper. Put another dot just below it. Turn back another page and do another dot a little lower.

Continue for the next 100 or so pages, leading the dot gradually back towards the 'is'. When you flick through the book, the dot will appear to move across the page until it points to the 'is'.

TO PERFORM

Ask for a volunteer, give them a calculator and say, *'Think of three numbers between 1 and 9 . . . Have you done that? Please enter them into the calculator as one number, biggest digit first, smallest digit last . . . Now press 'minus'.*

'Now enter the same numbers, but the other way round: smallest digit first and biggest digit last. Now press 'plus'. Look at the number on the screen and enter that number, the other way round. Press 'minus'. Enter '1038'. Press 'equals' and have a look at what it says.

'I would like you to find that in this book . . .' (hand them the book) *'. . . not at the bottom of*

the page, but in the text, among the words. Perhaps you think this will be hard? Never mind, the book will guide you to it. Simply flick through the book from the end backwards, and follow the dot . . .'

Watch as they do this, then ask, *'Done it? And does it say the same as your calculator?'* They will say, 'No – it's a word.' Then say to them, *'But what you have on the calculator is a word. Look!'* Turn the calculator over to reveal the word 'is' (51 upside down).

WHAT HAPPENED
The sum is a self-working trick. Whichever numbers are entered, the answer always comes to 51.

SEEING ROUND CORNERS

Have you noticed how easy it is to watch TV even when you're sitting way over to one side? The picture is squashed right up, but part of your brain can calculate what it would look like if you were seeing it from in front – and that's what you watch. It's a part of the brain you can trick.

Have a look at this picture. Could you fit a penny on to the tabletop without touching any line? Try it out and see.

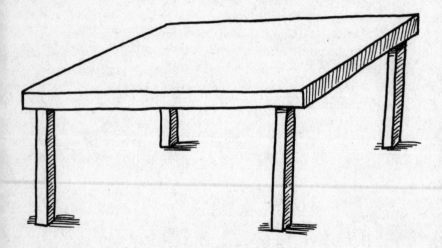

It looks possible, because although your eye sees a shape, your brain sees a table and imagines you putting the coin on top of that.

DOT'S AMAZING

How many colours do you think there are on a TV screen? In fact, there are only three! You can prove this by finding a patch of white on the screen and looking at it through a magnifying glass. You'll see that what you thought was white is actually made up of tiny red, green and blue dots. All the other colours you see are made up from different mixes of these basic colours.

So how many colours are there in the world? Only three?

When Issac Newton had finished working out the laws that control the entire universe, he spent a little time playing with light. He was the first to successfully split sunlight up into its different colours. Previously, people had found that if they shone sunlight through a prism on to a white screen, the beam of white light had a rainbow fringe.

But they had missed the real magic. Newton found
it by doing the simplest thing: he moved the screen farther
away from the prism. The white beam disappeared
completely, to be replaced by a rainbow. A miracle!
Newton could hardly believe his eyes. Where had the
white light gone? There was only one answer, incredible
though it seemed. Newton slipped another prism into the
path of the rainbow and put a screen behind. The rainbow
colours combined again to make white. This was magic!

Newton wrote a famous book about light which tried to
explain this magic scientifically. But although his theories
were based in rigorous experiments and cast iron facts, he
still had the remains of the old medieval alchemists about
him. He described seven colours in the rainbox: red, orange,
yellow, green, blue, indigo and violet. But if you've ever had
trouble telling indigo from violet, you're in good company.
Newton himself actually found only six colours, but among

religious and mystical people six was known as the number of the Devil. Because Newton was still pretty superstitious, that made him nervous. Seven, however, was a holy number, so seven colours there had to be! So, if Newton described *seven* colours, and if we can actually see *six*, and if the TV can manage with only *three*, how many are there really? The answer is: trillions and trillions! Visible light is a small section of a huge spread of **electromagnetic radiation**, which includes: radio waves, x-rays, heat rays, cosmic rays, and microwaves. Nowadays we have devices which can 'see' all these other waves, but our poor humble eyes can only detect a tiny sliver in the

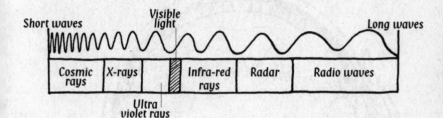

Short waves   Visible light   Long waves

| Cosmic rays | X-rays | | Infra-red rays | Radar | Radio waves |

Ultra violet rays

middle of the range. Just think, if our eyes had a wider range, we could *watch* music on the radio!

Even in that narrow band of ours there are an infinite number of 'colours', each blending seamlessly with the next. The reason we see such a lumpy picture, with those narrow strips of bright yellow, red and blue and so on, is because of the way our eyes are built.

EYES

There are four kinds of light-detecting cells in the back of the eye. Three of them, called **cones**, detect colours. The other sort, called **rods**, only see black and white, but they're useful because they can work in very dim light. That's why in the dark everything looks black, white and grey! The cones are concentrated in the middle of the eye, with the rods towards the outside. This means that at the edge of

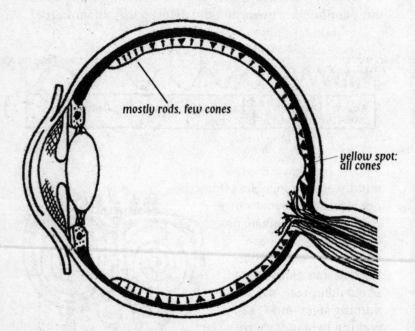

mostly rods, few cones

yellow spot: all cones

your vision, you are seeing things only in black and white, even on the brightest day. This may seem too unbelievable; you need proof – which you can get very quickly . . .

PERIPHERAL VISION

Use some felt-tip pens to draw different coloured lines on some pieces of paper. Shuffle the pieces and select one, without looking at it. Now stare fixedly forward and hold the paper just out of view, at the side of your head. Move it round slowly until you can just detect the line. Can you tell what colour it is?

Meanwhile, the cones concentrate on three colours – red, blue and green, exactly the same as the colours pumped out by the TV. The chemicals insides these cones vary slightly. The blue cones, for instance, can work in dimmer light than the red and green ones, which is why in the late evening everything looks blue before it goes black and grey. The red and yellow cones react stronger in bright light, which is why warning signs and flashing lights are more visible if they're red, orange or yellow.

We can do some magic with the spectrum of colours which sits above our head all day – the sky.

MULTICOLOURED MILK

This shows you how the sky changes colour through the day.

THE EFFECT
A glass of water changes colour from blue to red, just by adding milk.

YOU NEED
- Dark room
- Torch
- Big glass of water
- Milk
- Black background

TO PERFORM
Position the glass of water in front of the black background. Ask your audience some daft questions, such as, 'What colour is water? What colour is milk? Did you say orange? Did I hear blue?'

Show them the blue. Put a drop or two of milk in the water and shine the torch through the side of the glass. The cloudy mixture will look blue against the black background.

Put some more milk in the glass and shine the torch again. Now, if the light beam is at the right angle, you can clearly see orange.

WHAT HAPPENED

The light was scattered by the particles of milk in the water, just as daylight is scattered by particles, such as dust, in the atmosphere. Light at the blue end of the spectrum is scattered more easily than the red end, so during the day, blue light bounces around the sky and seems to come from all around, i.e. the sky looks blue. In the evening, the Sun is at a flatter angle and its light passes through more of the atmosphere (which you mimicked by putting more milk in the water), so the blue light is scattered clean away and only red light gets through to us.

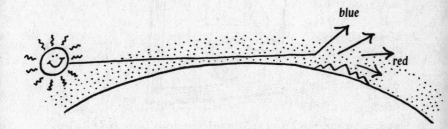

The great painter, JMW Turner, painted a series of brilliantly colourful sunsets in the 1840s. Recent research has discovered that at this time there was a huge volcanic eruption on the other side of the planet. The volcano spewed millions of tons of dust into the upper atmosphere, which was carried all around the globe, giving Europe a series of spectacular sunsets for Turner to paint.

CHAPTER EIGHT

ON REFLECTION

Hold a mirror up in front of a mirror. What you can see is a reflection of a reflection of a reflection of a reflection of a reflection . . .

Has it ever worried you that a mirror does only half its job? It reverses your right and left sides, but doesn't reverse your top and bottom. Many sleek scientists have had to pause to reflect on this matter.

Of course, what you see is not what everyone else gets. Since your left and right sides are reversed, you see a different you to the you that we see, if you see what I mean.

'But', I hear you plead, 'surely it makes no difference which way round I am, since both sides are the same'.

How wrong you are!

TWO YOU

Ｆor this you need a small pocket mirror and a full frontal photograph of your face. Place the mirror on your mug shot, as in the picture, with the edge running down the middle of your nose.

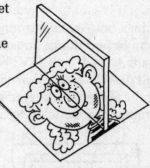

Look at the face formed by the reflection of the right side and compare it with the face formed by the left side's reflection. They are quite different, aren't they?

To see yourself as others see you, place the mirror at right angles to another mirror. That strange face you're looking at is your own.

SYMMETRY

If one side of something is exactly the same as the other side, it is said to be **symmetrical**. How many symmetrical things can you find around the living room? It can be quite hard to find things that are completely and utterly symmetrical. Is the TV? What about a pair of scissors? Is a roll of sellotape symmetrical? A chair? How many letters of the alphabet are symmetrical? How many are symmetrical both left to right *and* top to bottom?

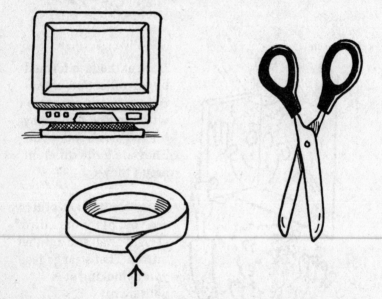

A perfectly round, blank sphere has perfect symmetry about the centre point. How many lines of symmetry has a marble? A bottle? A piece of paper? How many natural things are symmetrical? Trees, birds, snails? Man-made things tend to be symmetrical because it's easier to make them that way. Do you think the same laws apply in nature?

FLOATING ART

For this illusion you will need an unwanted paperback book, some Post-its, and some blutac.

Remove the back cover of the book and stick the back page to the mirror, as in the picture. It will look as if the book is floating in the air. Then cut some shapes out of Post-its and stick them to the mirror – a half-bird, a half-person jumping or diving, one side of an aeroplane, a semi-circle of flowers. The mirror will provide the rest.

LESS IS MORE
OR LESS THE SAME

Simple pocket mirrors are the size they are for a special
reason: they are just the right size to let you see your
entire face, and not much more. The way scientists illustrate
this is to draw a diagram showing the path of light from an
object into the eye

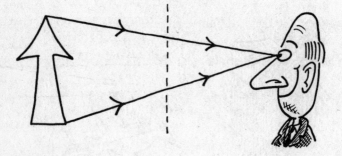

The image in the eye is tiny. The object is of course
full-size. So half-way between the object and the eye, the
image is half-size. And a mirror is bound to be half-way
between the object (your face) and eye. So your reflection
is exactly half-size.There's some magic to be done with
this . . .

Show someone the mirror and ask them how much of
themselves they can see in it. Now ask them how much
they think they'll see if the mirror is the other side of the
room. They will probably imagine that they can see more
of themselves.

Hold the mirror for them, across the other side of the room. They'll be surprised that they can see exactly the same amount of themselves. Why? Because however far away you put your mirror, it is still half-way between the object (your face) and your eye, so the reflection cannot help being half-size.

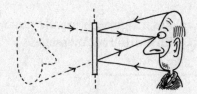

close to mirror

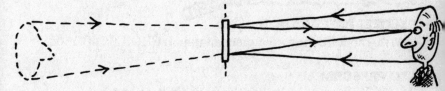

far away from mirror

CHOICE DICE

In this trick the main performer is the mirror.

THE EFFECT
The magician makes a sign turn upside down and inside out, ending up with a different message.

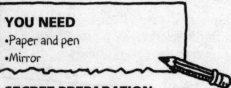

YOU NEED
•Paper and pen
•Mirror

SECRET PREPARATION
Write the following on a piece of paper: CHOICE DICE 50c.

TO PERFORM
Say to your audience, *'Las Vegas, in America, is the gambling capital of the world. The streets are full of shops selling gambling aids – cards, casino chips, trouser pockets with ready-made holes in . . . and dice. Smarty Pants walks into a gambling shop and says, "I see from your sign . . ."'* (hold up the sign) *'" . . . that you're selling dice. I'd like one, please."*

'The shopkeeper says, "Certainly, sir. That will be 50 cents, please."
"But your sign says 20 cents."
"Our sign most defininitely says 50 cents, sir. There it is, sir. See for yourself."
"That says 20 cents."
"Well, sir, if you can prove to me that the sign says 20 cents,

then you can have the dice for 10 cents!"
'Smarty Pants says, "OK. First of all, you're looking at it wrong. You should be looking at it in the mirror . . ."' (Let everyone look at the sign in the mirror.)

'The shopkeeper replies, "Well, sir – and with all due respect – that still doesn't say 20 cents."
' Smarty announces, "That's because the sign is upside down!"' (Turn the sign round. The reflection now reads: CHOICE DICE 20c.)

WHAT HAPPENED

When you invert the sign you flip the image both top to bottom and left to right. In the mirror, the image flips left to right (back to where it comes from) but not top to bottom. So the lettering is still upside down. But every letter of that sign is symmetrical top to bottom, except the 5. So the 5 becomes 2, while the rest apparently stay the same.

So I hope that makes everything absolutely clear for you.

And Finally . . . A Big Magical Excuse

How To Get Away With Being Late For Science Lessons

Next time you're late for science, tell the teacher this.

> 'I'm sorry I'm late. I set off in a straight line for the classroom at a steady speed, but air resistance dragged me back, gravity pulled me down, and friction slowed me up, to say nothing of the effort of combating inertia at the corners.'

Teacher will be so pleased with your scientific answer that they'll ask you to be late every day.

LIST OF MAGIC TRICKS